THIS PLANNER
Belongs To:

_____

DATE:

ALL ABOUT *me*

1. What are you most grateful for in your life?

Keeping track of what you're most grateful for will keep you focused on the blessings in your life. Consider the many reasons you have to be grateful BELOW:

2. What do you love about yourself?

Self love isn't always easy but writing down what you're most proud of will help clear your mind of the criticism and negativity you may feel.

3. Where is your happy place?

Where do you feel most at peace? Do you have a favorite spot that allows you to refocus your energy, find inner peace and feel happiness? Describe your happy place.

DATE:

ALL ABOUT *me*

4. What do you enjoy doing?

What are your favorite activities where you are able to boost your mood and free your mind? This could be a hobby or physical activity, or perhaps something entirely different.

5. Who can you rely on?

Describe the people in your life that you can count on when things get tough. Who do you feel closest to?

6. How can you improve your life?

What changes can you make that will ultimately improve your life and give you joy? This could be career or personal related. Please share your thoughts below.

DATE:

ALL ABOUT *me*

7. My greatest accomplishments are:

What are some of the things you are most proud of?

8. What do you wish others knew about you?

What do you wish others knew about who you really are? What do you feel others overlook?

9. What are your greatest aspirations?

Whether it be personal, career or family goals, list them below.

DEAR FUTURE Self...

FOCUS ON YOUR VISION OF A HAPPY FUTURE

FAMILY GOALS	CAREER GOALS
SELF CARE	RELATIONSHIP
HEALTH GOALS	FRIENDSHIPS
PERSONAL	FINANCIAL
TRAVEL	PASSIONS
NEW SKILLS	OTHER
5 YEARS FROM NOW	10 YEARS FROM NOW

COPING *Strategies*

COPING SKILLS

Write down the different ways you feel about yourself as well as personal situations, and how you can better manage and cope with self-doubt and negative feelings.

WHEN I'M FEELING...	I WILL MANAGE IT BY...
WHEN I'M FEELING...	I WILL MANAGE IT BY...
WHEN I'M FEELING...	I WILL MANAGE IT BY...
WHEN I'M FEELING...	I WILL MANAGE IT BY...
WHEN I'M FEELING...	I WILL MANAGE IT BY...
WHEN I'M FEELING...	I WILL MANAGE IT BY...
WHEN I'M FEELING...	I WILL MANAGE IT BY...

OTHER IDEAS / NOTES

DATE:

ANXIETY debrief

Describe a situation where you felt anxious:

What were the physical symptoms you experienced?

Did you face the situation or remove yourself from it?

How did you cope with this anxiety? Do you believe your thoughts and reactions were rational?

ANXIETY *levels*

Use the chart below to rate your level of anxiety when facing various situations by coloring the boxes:

SITUATION: Meeting Someone New

ANXIETY LEVEL

DO YOU: Face this fear   Avoid this situation

SITUATION: Going to the grocery store

ANXIETY LEVEL

DO YOU: Face this fear   Avoid this situation

SITUATION: Stating your opinion when potentially controversial or opposing.

ANXIETY LEVEL

DO YOU: Face this fear   Avoid this situation

SITUATION: Stand up for yourself when treated unfairly or poorly.

ANXIETY LEVEL

DO YOU: Face this fear   Avoid this situation

SITUATION: Spending time alone with friends and/or family.

ANXIETY LEVEL

DO YOU: Face this fear   Avoid this situation

SITUATION: Being watched/observed when doing something/completing a task or activity.

ANXIETY LEVEL

DO YOU: Face this fear   Avoid this situation

UNDERSTANDING *anxiety*

Understanding the origin of your anxiety will help you learn new ways to manage your responses.

SITUATION: Meeting Someone New **WHAT IS YOUR BIGGEST FEAR WHEN FACING THIS SITUATION?**

SITUATION: Going to the grocery store **WHAT IS YOUR BIGGEST FEAR WHEN FACING THIS SITUATION?**

SITUATION: Stating your opinion. **WHAT IS YOUR BIGGEST FEAR WHEN FACING THIS SITUATION?**

SITUATION: Stand up for yourself. **WHAT IS YOUR BIGGEST FEAR WHEN FACING THIS SITUATION?**

SITUATION: Spending time alone with friends. **WHAT IS YOUR BIGGEST FEAR WHEN FACING THIS SITUATION?**

SITUATION: Being watched/observed. **WHAT IS YOUR BIGGEST FEAR WHEN FACING THIS SITUATION?**

GRATEFUL *Life*

What are the things you are most grateful for? Spend time self-reflecting on the many blessings in your life. Shift your focus on gratitude and rid yourself of negative emotions and toxic thoughts.

1	2	3
4	5	6
7	8	9
10	11	12

HAPPINESS Is...

Complete the following sentences to refocus your mind on the joys in your life:

I FEEL MOST RELAXED WHEN:

I AM LESS STRESSED WHEN:

MY STRENGTHS ARE:

I AM A GOOD FRIEND BECAUSE:

I AM MOST EXCITED BY:

I AM MOST FOCUSED WHEN:

I FEEL MOST APPRECIATED WHEN:

I AM MOST MOTIVATED WHEN:

THOUGHTS Tracker

MONITORING YOUR THOUGHTS & FEELINGS

MONDAY'S THOUGHTS

TUESDAY'S THOUGHTS

WEDNESDAY'S THOUGHTS

THURSDAY'S THOUGHTS

FRIDAY'S THOUGHTS

SATURDAY'S THOUGHTS

SUNDAY'S THOUGHTS

TRANSFORMING *Thoughts*

TRANSFORMING NEGATIVE THOUGHTS

We all deal with negative thoughts and self-doubt. Use this space to keep track of those feelings and focus on how you can replace them with positive thoughts that promote self-growth.

NEGATIVE THOUGHT	REPLACEMENT THOUGHT
NEGATIVE THOUGHT	REPLACEMENT THOUGHT
NEGATIVE THOUGHT	REPLACEMENT THOUGHT
NEGATIVE THOUGHT	REPLACEMENT THOUGHT
NEGATIVE THOUGHT	REPLACEMENT THOUGHT
NEGATIVE THOUGHT	REPLACEMENT THOUGHT

PERSONAL REFLECTIONS

SELF AWARENESS *Chart*

CHALLENGE NEGATIVE THOUGHTS AND FEELINGS

It's easy to get lost in our own headspace so it's important that you question any negative feelings so you can sort through your emotions effectively. Use this worksheet to document your progress.

THOUGHT

IS THE THOUGHT VALID?

HOW DO YOU REACT TO THIS NEGATIVE THOUGHT?

WHAT COULD YOU DO TO AVOID FEELING THIS WAY?

THOUGHTS & REFLECTIONS

MOOD *Chart*

Use the wheel below to document your moods every month.
Use 3 different colors to represent positive, negative or neutral emotions.

☐ POSITIVE ☐ NEGATIVE ☐ NEUTRAL

MONTH:

1, 2, 3, 4, 5, 6, 7, 8, 9, 10, 11, 12, 13, 14, 15, 16, 17, 18, 19, 20, 21, 22, 23, 24, 25, 26, 27, 28, 29, 30, 31

SLEEP *Tracker*

MONTH: _____

Sleep plays a major factor in our ability to cope with anxiety and depression. Keep track of your sleep pattern in order to determine how the amount of rest may be affecting your mental health.

DAY	HOURS SLEPT	QUALITY OF SLEEP	THOUGHTS
1			
2			
3			
4			
5			
6			
7			
8			
9			
10			
11			
12			
13			
14			
15			
16			
17			
18			
19			
20			
21			
22			
23			
24			
25			
26			
27			
28			
29			
30			
31			

LIFE Assessment

SUMMARIZE HOW YOU **FEEL** ABOUT YOUR LIFE

TOP 3 AREAS OF YOUR LIFE YOU'D LIKE TO **IMPROVE**

01

02

03

3 WAYS YOU CAN **ACCOMPLISH** YOUR LIFE GOALS

MONTH: _____

TRIGGER *Tracker*

Keep track of experiences that generate negative thoughts and emotions.

DATE   INCIDENT   REACTION

GRATEFUL *Heart*

MONTH:

DAY · TODAY I AM GRATEFUL FOR:

1
2
3
4
5
6
7
8
9
10
11
12
13
14
15
16
17
18
19
20
21
22
23
24
25
26
27
28
29
30
31

SELF Improvement

WHAT ARE YOUR SELF SABOTAGE HABITS?

Eliminate Negative Habits

Create Positive Habits

HOW CAN YOU IMPROVE YOUR MENTAL HEALTH?

What Key Areas Need Work?

What Are Some Steps You Can Take?

ANALYZING THE PEOPLE IN YOUR LIFE

Who Are The Negative Influences?

Who Are The Positive Influences?

HOW DO I HOLD MYSELF ACCOUNTABLE?

What I Know I'm Responsible For

Who Helps Keep Me Accountable?

SELF CARE *Ideas*

NURTURE YOUR MIND

- Discover new hobbies
- Read a book
- Take a road trip
- Keep a journal
- Talk to a friend
- Follow inspiring people
- Challenge yourself
- Be grateful
- Call an old friend
- Try something new

FEED YOUR SPIRIT

- Have "me-time"
- Listen to music
- Read poetry
- Write "future-self"
- Paint
- Meditate

TAKE CARE OF YOUR BODY

- Eat healthy
- Start a workout plan
- Get enough sleep
- Stay hydrated
- Yoga

Ideas

SELF CARE *Planner*

Self-care involves taking care of yourself emotionally, mentally and physically.
Create a self-care plan by adding activities to the categories below.

MENTAL SELF-CARE

PHYSICAL SELF-CARE (GET ACTIVE)

EMOTIONAL SELF-CARE

DAILY HABITS (SLEEP, ETC.)

REACH OUT (SOCIALIZE)

SUPPORT NETWORK

OTHER:

SELF CARE *Tracker*

Self care is an important step in managing anxiety and depression. It helps us recharge, reset and nurtures our mind and soul. Focus on incorporating one self-care activity into your daily life.

MONTH: _____

THOUGHT *Log*

Keep track of negative thoughts so you can learn how to control irrational responses and triggers.

DATE	INCIDENT	INITIAL REACTION	RATIONAL REACTION

PERSONAL Wins

MONTH:

It's important to celebrate both minor and major wins when it comes to your mental health and the coping strategies you've learned along the way. You've come a long way!

2 RECENT WINS

TOP 3 MILESTONES

1.
2.
3.

3 THINGS I'VE LEARNED ABOUT MYSELF OVER THE LAST YEAR

PERSONAL REFLECTIONS	HOW I'VE LEARNED TO COPE WITH EMOTIONS

NOTES

PERSONAL Rewards

MONTH:

Make sure to reward yourself for accomplishments throughout your journey. Whether it's a visit to your favorite restaurant, a bubble bath or an evening with friends, it's important to celebrate your progress every step of the way.

IDEAS FOR PERSONAL REWARDS

1	2
3	4
5	6

HOW I FELT BEFORE	HOW I REWARDED MYSELF	HOW I FELT AFTER REWARD

NOTES	PERSONAL REFLECTIONS/THOUGHTS

ANXIETY Tracker

Document the days when you experienced anxiety. This page includes a 3-week tracker.

ANXIETY LEVELS (1-MILD, 10 SEVERE)

Day													Notes
MON	01	02	03	04	05	06	07	08	09	10	11	12	
TUE	01	02	03	04	05	06	07	08	09	10	11	12	
WED	01	02	03	04	05	06	07	08	09	10	11	12	
THU	01	02	03	04	05	06	07	08	09	10	11	12	
FRI	01	02	03	04	05	06	07	08	09	10	11	12	
SAT	01	02	03	04	05	06	07	08	09	10	11	12	
SUN	01	02	03	04	05	06	07	08	09	10	11	12	
MON	01	02	03	04	05	06	07	08	09	10	11	12	
TUE	01	02	03	04	05	06	07	08	09	10	11	12	
WED	01	02	03	04	05	06	07	08	09	10	11	12	
THU	01	02	03	04	05	06	07	08	09	10	11	12	
FRI	01	02	03	04	05	06	07	08	09	10	11	12	
SAT	01	02	03	04	05	06	07	08	09	10	11	12	
SUN	01	02	03	04	05	06	07	08	09	10	11	12	
MON	01	02	03	04	05	06	07	08	09	10	11	12	
TUE	01	02	03	04	05	06	07	08	09	10	11	12	
WED	01	02	03	04	05	06	07	08	09	10	11	12	
THU	01	02	03	04	05	06	07	08	09	10	11	12	
FRI	01	02	03	04	05	06	07	08	09	10	11	12	
SAT	01	02	03	04	05	06	07	08	09	10	11	12	
SUN	01	02	03	04	05	06	07	08	09	10	11	12	

DATE I STARTED TRACKING:

DEPRESSION *Tracker*

Document the days when you experienced depression. This page includes a 3-week tracker.

DEPRESSION LEVELS (1-MILD, 10 SEVERE)

Day													NOTES:
MON	01	02	03	04	05	06	07	08	09	10	11	12	
TUE	01	02	03	04	05	06	07	08	09	10	11	12	
WED	01	02	03	04	05	06	07	08	09	10	11	12	
THU	01	02	03	04	05	06	07	08	09	10	11	12	
FRI	01	02	03	04	05	06	07	08	09	10	11	12	
SAT	01	02	03	04	05	06	07	08	09	10	11	12	
SUN	01	02	03	04	05	06	07	08	09	10	11	12	
MON	01	02	03	04	05	06	07	08	09	10	11	12	
TUE	01	02	03	04	05	06	07	08	09	10	11	12	
WED	01	02	03	04	05	06	07	08	09	10	11	12	
THU	01	02	03	04	05	06	07	08	09	10	11	12	
FRI	01	02	03	04	05	06	07	08	09	10	11	12	
SAT	01	02	03	04	05	06	07	08	09	10	11	12	
SUN	01	02	03	04	05	06	07	08	09	10	11	12	
MON	01	02	03	04	05	06	07	08	09	10	11	12	
TUE	01	02	03	04	05	06	07	08	09	10	11	12	
WED	01	02	03	04	05	06	07	08	09	10	11	12	
THU	01	02	03	04	05	06	07	08	09	10	11	12	
FRI	01	02	03	04	05	06	07	08	09	10	11	12	
SAT	01	02	03	04	05	06	07	08	09	10	11	12	
SUN	01	02	03	04	05	06	07	08	09	10	11	12	

DATE I STARTED TRACKING:

RESET *your mind*

We can't always control the way our thoughts but we can learn to transform negative feelings into positive ones and control our reactions and impulses. Use the chart below to start the process.

WHEN I FEEL LIKE:		I WILL TRY TO CONTROL BY REACTIONS BY:
	}	
	}	
	}	
	}	
	}	
	}	
	}	
	}	
	}	
	}	
	}	
	}	
	}	

NOTES & REFLECTIONS   DOODLES & SCRIBBLES

LOVE Yourself

STEP 1: MAKE YOURSELF A PRIORITY

It's important to always put yourself first by listening to your inner voice. Let it guide you in eliminating toxic people and negative sources. Don't be afraid to distance yourself from people and places that make you feel unhappy or who don't support your journey.

STEP 2: FACE YOUR FEARS

Don't be afraid to confront your fears and self-doubt. Why do you feel unworthy at times? What are you most worried about?

STEP 3: BE ACCOUNTABLE

Hold yourself accountable for the things you can control and change. There are things in your life only you can change.

STEP 4: FORGIVE YOURSELF

Let go of past mistakes – you can't go back in time. We all have regrets and while it's important to hold yourself accountable for mistakes, you can only truly heal when you learn to forgive yourself. Free your mind so it can focus on a better you and a happier tomorrow.

STEP 5: ACCEPT WHERE YOU ARE IN YOUR JOURNEY

Don't allow yourself to grow frustrated that you aren't able to race towards the finish line. Your journey will take time so give yourself permission to fail while also learning to accept where you are right now. Take it one day at a time. You owe it to yourself to stay focused on the road ahead while celebrating every milestone along the way.

Write down your thoughts, reflections and ideas below:

Thoughts

SELF CARE *Focus*

TOP 3 SELF-CARE ACTIVITIES

HOW THEY MAKE ME FEEL

01

02

03

OTHER SELF-CARE ACTIVITIES THAT MAKE ME HAPPY

01

02

03

FAVORITE QUOTES/WORDS OF ENCOURAGEMENT

TRIGGER Sources

Discover what causes emotional pain and negative thoughts in your life.

Describe the negative reaction/response you would like to overcome:

Consider the aspects of your life below and write down how each category can cause the above trigger.

PERSONAL

PEOPLE

PLACES

SITUATIONS

Think about the different ways you can overcome your triggers when dealing with each category. How can you better control your reactions and manage frustrating situations?

HAPPINESS Tracker

Keep track of how often you feel happy and calm and what you did to minimize negative responses.

DATE:

DATE:

HAPPINESS RATING:    HAPPINESS RATING:

DATE:

DATE:

HAPPINESS RATING:    HAPPINESS RATING:

DATE:

DATE:

HAPPINESS RATING:    HAPPINESS RATING:

DAILY *Reflection*

DATE:

HOW I FEEL TODAY

MY GREATEST CHALLENGE

MOOD TRACKER:

MORNING:

EVENING:

I FELT HAPPY WHEN:

I FELT EXCITED WHEN:

I FELT ENERGIZED WHEN:

Today's Highlights

What I'm Grateful For Today

DAILY *Awareness*

MONTH:

M T W T F S S

HOW I'M FEELING TODAY

3 WORDS TO DESCRIBE MY DAY

STRUGGLES

HIGHLIGHT OF MY DAY

DAILY ACCOMPLISHMENTS

DATE:

DAILY *Reflection*

HOW I FEEL TODAY　　　　　　　　　　　　**MY GREATEST CHALLENGE**

MOOD TRACKER:

MORNING:　　　　　　　　　　**EVENING:**

I FELT HAPPY WHEN:　　　**I FELT EXCITED WHEN:**　　　**I FELT ENERGIZED WHEN:**

Today's Highlights

What I'm Grateful For Today

DAILY *Awareness*

MONTH:

M T W T F S S

HOW I'M FEELING TODAY

3 WORDS TO DESCRIBE MY DAY   **STRUGGLES**

HIGHLIGHT OF MY DAY

DAILY ACCOMPLISHMENTS

DAILY *Reflection*

DATE:

HOW I FEEL TODAY

MY GREATEST CHALLENGE

MOOD TRACKER:

MORNING:

EVENING:

I FELT HAPPY WHEN:

I FELT EXCITED WHEN:

I FELT ENERGIZED WHEN:

Today's Highlights

What I'm Grateful For Today

DAILY *Awareness*

MONTH:

M T W T F S S

HOW I'M FEELING TODAY

3 WORDS TO DESCRIBE MY DAY

STRUGGLES

HIGHLIGHT OF MY DAY

DAILY ACCOMPLISHMENTS

DAILY *Reflection*

DATE:

HOW I FEEL TODAY

MY GREATEST CHALLENGE

MOOD TRACKER:

MORNING:

EVENING:

I FELT HAPPY WHEN:

I FELT EXCITED WHEN:

I FELT ENERGIZED WHEN:

Today's Highlights

What I'm Grateful For Today

DAILY *Awareness*

MONTH:

M T W T F S S

HOW I'M FEELING TODAY

3 WORDS TO DESCRIBE MY DAY

STRUGGLES

HIGHLIGHT OF MY DAY

DAILY ACCOMPLISHMENTS

DAILY *Reflection*

DATE:

HOW I FEEL TODAY

MY GREATEST CHALLENGE

MOOD TRACKER:

MORNING:

EVENING:

I FELT HAPPY WHEN:

I FELT EXCITED WHEN:

I FELT ENERGIZED WHEN:

Today's Highlights

What I'm Grateful For Today

DAILY *Awareness*

MONTH:

M T W T F S S

HOW I'M FEELING TODAY

3 WORDS TO DESCRIBE MY DAY

STRUGGLES

HIGHLIGHT OF MY DAY

DAILY ACCOMPLISHMENTS

DATE:

DAILY Reflection

HOW I FEEL TODAY **MY GREATEST CHALLENGE**

MOOD TRACKER:

MORNING: **EVENING:**

I FELT HAPPY WHEN: **I FELT EXCITED WHEN:** **I FELT ENERGIZED WHEN:**

Today's Highlights

What I'm Grateful For Today

DAILY *Awareness*

MONTH:

M T W T F S S

HOW I'M FEELING TODAY

3 WORDS TO DESCRIBE MY DAY   **STRUGGLES**

HIGHLIGHT OF MY DAY

DAILY ACCOMPLISHMENTS

DATE:

DAILY Reflection

HOW I FEEL TODAY

MY GREATEST CHALLENGE

MOOD TRACKER:

MORNING:

EVENING:

I FELT HAPPY WHEN:

I FELT EXCITED WHEN:

I FELT ENERGIZED WHEN:

Today's Highlights

What I'm Grateful For Today

DAILY Awareness

MONTH:

M T W T F S S

HOW I'M FEELING TODAY

3 WORDS TO DESCRIBE MY DAY

STRUGGLES

HIGHLIGHT OF MY DAY

DAILY ACCOMPLISHMENTS

POST Therapy Chart

DATE:

SUMMARY/OVERVIEW OF THERAPY SESSION

WHAT WE DISCUSSED

HOW IT MADE ME FEEL

WHAT I LEARNED

WHAT I WANT TO DISCUSS NEXT

Rate your session to keep track of progress.

WEEKLY Assessment

	SLEEP	MOOD	POSITIVES	NEGATIVES
MONDAY				
TUESDAY				
WEDNESDAY				
THURSDAY				
FRIDAY				
SATURADY				
SUNDAY				

WEEKLY *Reflections*

Monday

Tuesday

Wednesday

Thursday

Friday

Saturday

Sunday

DAILY *Reflection*

DATE:

HOW I FEEL TODAY

MY GREATEST CHALLENGE

MOOD TRACKER:

MORNING:

EVENING:

I FELT HAPPY WHEN:

I FELT EXCITED WHEN:

I FELT ENERGIZED WHEN:

Today's Highlights

What I'm Grateful For Today

DAILY *Awareness*

MONTH:

M T W T F S S

HOW I'M FEELING TODAY

3 WORDS TO DESCRIBE MY DAY

STRUGGLES

HIGHLIGHT OF MY DAY

DAILY ACCOMPLISHMENTS

DAILY *Reflection*

DATE:

HOW I FEEL TODAY

MY GREATEST CHALLENGE

MOOD TRACKER:

MORNING:

EVENING:

I FELT HAPPY WHEN:

I FELT EXCITED WHEN:

I FELT ENERGIZED WHEN:

Today's Highlights

What I'm Grateful For Today

DAILY *Awareness*

MONTH:

M T W T F S S

HOW I'M FEELING TODAY

3 WORDS TO DESCRIBE MY DAY

STRUGGLES

HIGHLIGHT OF MY DAY

DAILY ACCOMPLISHMENTS

DAILY *Reflection*

DATE:

HOW I FEEL TODAY

MY GREATEST CHALLENGE

MOOD TRACKER:

MORNING:

EVENING:

I FELT HAPPY WHEN:

I FELT EXCITED WHEN:

I FELT ENERGIZED WHEN:

Today's Highlights

What I'm Grateful For Today

DAILY Awareness

MONTH:

M T W T F S S

HOW I'M FEELING TODAY

3 WORDS TO DESCRIBE MY DAY **STRUGGLES**

HIGHLIGHT OF MY DAY

DAILY ACCOMPLISHMENTS

DAILY *Reflection*

DATE:

HOW I FEEL TODAY

MY GREATEST CHALLENGE

MOOD TRACKER:

MORNING:

EVENING:

I FELT HAPPY WHEN:

I FELT EXCITED WHEN:

I FELT ENERGIZED WHEN:

Today's Highlights

What I'm Grateful For Today

DAILY *Awareness*

MONTH:

M T W T F S S

HOW I'M FEELING TODAY

3 WORDS TO DESCRIBE MY DAY

STRUGGLES

HIGHLIGHT OF MY DAY

DAILY ACCOMPLISHMENTS

DATE:

DAILY *Reflection*

HOW I FEEL TODAY **MY GREATEST CHALLENGE**

MOOD TRACKER:

MORNING: EVENING:

I FELT HAPPY WHEN: **I FELT EXCITED WHEN:** **I FELT ENERGIZED WHEN:**

Today's Highlights

What I'm Grateful For Today

DAILY Awareness

MONTH:

M T W T F S S

HOW I'M FEELING TODAY

3 WORDS TO DESCRIBE MY DAY

STRUGGLES

HIGHLIGHT OF MY DAY

DAILY ACCOMPLISHMENTS

DATE:

DAILY *Reflection*

HOW I FEEL TODAY

MY GREATEST CHALLENGE

MOOD TRACKER:

MORNING:

EVENING:

I FELT HAPPY WHEN:

I FELT EXCITED WHEN:

I FELT ENERGIZED WHEN:

Today's Highlights

What I'm Grateful For Today

DAILY *Awareness*

MONTH:

M T W T F S S

HOW I'M FEELING TODAY

3 WORDS TO DESCRIBE MY DAY

STRUGGLES

HIGHLIGHT OF MY DAY

DAILY ACCOMPLISHMENTS

DAILY *Reflection*

DATE:

HOW I FEEL TODAY

MY GREATEST CHALLENGE

MOOD TRACKER:

MORNING:

EVENING:

I FELT HAPPY WHEN:

I FELT EXCITED WHEN:

I FELT ENERGIZED WHEN:

Today's Highlights

What I'm Grateful For Today

DAILY *Awareness*

MONTH:

M T W T F S S

HOW I'M FEELING TODAY

3 WORDS TO DESCRIBE MY DAY

STRUGGLES

HIGHLIGHT OF MY DAY

DAILY ACCOMPLISHMENTS

POST Therapy Chart

DATE:

SUMMARY/OVERVIEW OF THERAPY SESSION

WHAT WE DISCUSSED

HOW IT MADE ME FEEL

WHAT I LEARNED

WHAT I WANT TO DISCUSS NEXT

Rate your session to keep track of progress.

WEEKLY *Assessment*

	SLEEP	MOOD	POSITIVES	NEGATIVES
MONDAY				
TUESDAY				
WEDNESDAY				
THURSDAY				
FRIDAY				
SATURADY				
SUNDAY				

WEEKLY *Reflections*

Monday

Tuesday

Wednesday

Thursday

Friday

Saturday

Sunday

DAILY *Reflection*

DATE:

HOW I FEEL TODAY

MY GREATEST CHALLENGE

MOOD TRACKER:

MORNING:

EVENING:

I FELT HAPPY WHEN:

I FELT EXCITED WHEN:

I FELT ENERGIZED WHEN:

Today's Highlights

What I'm Grateful For Today

DAILY *Awareness*

MONTH:

M T W T F S S

HOW I'M FEELING TODAY

3 WORDS TO DESCRIBE MY DAY

STRUGGLES

HIGHLIGHT OF MY DAY

DAILY ACCOMPLISHMENTS

DAILY Reflection

DATE:

HOW I FEEL TODAY

MY GREATEST CHALLENGE

MOOD TRACKER:

MORNING:

EVENING:

I FELT HAPPY WHEN:

I FELT EXCITED WHEN:

I FELT ENERGIZED WHEN:

Today's Highlights

What I'm Grateful For Today

DAILY *Awareness*

MONTH:

M T W T F S S

HOW I'M FEELING TODAY

3 WORDS TO DESCRIBE MY DAY

STRUGGLES

HIGHLIGHT OF MY DAY

DAILY ACCOMPLISHMENTS

DATE:

DAILY *Reflection*

HOW I FEEL TODAY **MY GREATEST CHALLENGE**

MOOD TRACKER:

MORNING: **EVENING:**

I FELT HAPPY WHEN: **I FELT EXCITED WHEN:** **I FELT ENERGIZED WHEN:**

Today's Highlights

What I'm Grateful For Today

DAILY *Awareness*

MONTH:

M T W T F S S

HOW I'M FEELING TODAY

3 WORDS TO DESCRIBE MY DAY

STRUGGLES

HIGHLIGHT OF MY DAY

DAILY ACCOMPLISHMENTS

DATE:

DAILY *Reflection*

HOW I FEEL TODAY **MY GREATEST CHALLENGE**

MOOD TRACKER:

MORNING: EVENING:

I FELT HAPPY WHEN: I FELT EXCITED WHEN: I FELT ENERGIZED WHEN:

Today's Highlights

What I'm Grateful For Today

DAILY *Awareness*

MONTH:

M T W T F S S

HOW I'M FEELING TODAY

3 WORDS TO DESCRIBE MY DAY

STRUGGLES

HIGHLIGHT OF MY DAY

DAILY ACCOMPLISHMENTS

DAILY *Reflection*

DATE:

HOW I FEEL TODAY

MY GREATEST CHALLENGE

MOOD TRACKER:

MORNING:

EVENING:

I FELT HAPPY WHEN:

I FELT EXCITED WHEN:

I FELT ENERGIZED WHEN:

Today's Highlights

What I'm Grateful For Today

DAILY *Awareness*

MONTH:

M T W T F S S

HOW I'M FEELING TODAY

3 WORDS TO DESCRIBE MY DAY

STRUGGLES

HIGHLIGHT OF MY DAY

DAILY ACCOMPLISHMENTS

DATE:

DAILY Reflection

HOW I FEEL TODAY

MY GREATEST CHALLENGE

MOOD TRACKER:

MORNING:

EVENING:

I FELT HAPPY WHEN:

I FELT EXCITED WHEN:

I FELT ENERGIZED WHEN:

Today's Highlights

What I'm Grateful For Today

DAILY *Awareness*

MONTH:

M T W T F S S

HOW I'M FEELING TODAY

3 WORDS TO DESCRIBE MY DAY

STRUGGLES

HIGHLIGHT OF MY DAY

DAILY ACCOMPLISHMENTS

DAILY *Reflection*

DATE:

HOW I FEEL TODAY **MY GREATEST CHALLENGE**

MOOD TRACKER:

MORNING: EVENING:

I FELT HAPPY WHEN: I FELT EXCITED WHEN: I FELT ENERGIZED WHEN:

Today's Highlights

What I'm Grateful For Today

ANXIETY Tracker

Document the days when you experienced anxiety. This page includes a 3-week tracker.

ANXIETY LEVELS (1-MILD, 10 SEVERE)

Day	01	02	03	04	05	06	07	08	09	10	11	12
MON	01	02	03	04	05	06	07	08	09	10	11	12
TUE	01	02	03	04	05	06	07	08	09	10	11	12
WED	01	02	03	04	05	06	07	08	09	10	11	12
THU	01	02	03	04	05	06	07	08	09	10	11	12
FRI	01	02	03	04	05	06	07	08	09	10	11	12
SAT	01	02	03	04	05	06	07	08	09	10	11	12
SUN	01	02	03	04	05	06	07	08	09	10	11	12
MON	01	02	03	04	05	06	07	08	09	10	11	12
TUE	01	02	03	04	05	06	07	08	09	10	11	12
WED	01	02	03	04	05	06	07	08	09	10	11	12
THU	01	02	03	04	05	06	07	08	09	10	11	12
FRI	01	02	03	04	05	06	07	08	09	10	11	12
SAT	01	02	03	04	05	06	07	08	09	10	11	12
SUN	01	02	03	04	05	06	07	08	09	10	11	12
MON	01	02	03	04	05	06	07	08	09	10	11	12
TUE	01	02	03	04	05	06	07	08	09	10	11	12
WED	01	02	03	04	05	06	07	08	09	10	11	12
THU	01	02	03	04	05	06	07	08	09	10	11	12
FRI	01	02	03	04	05	06	07	08	09	10	11	12
SAT	01	02	03	04	05	06	07	08	09	10	11	12
SUN	01	02	03	04	05	06	07	08	09	10	11	12

NOTES:

DATE I STARTED TRACKING:

DEPRESSION Tracker

Document the days when you experienced depression. This page includes a 3-week tracker.

DEPRESSION LEVELS (1-MILD, 10 SEVERE)

Day	01	02	03	04	05	06	07	08	09	10	11	12
MON	01	02	03	04	05	06	07	08	09	10	11	12
TUE	01	02	03	04	05	06	07	08	09	10	11	12
WED	01	02	03	04	05	06	07	08	09	10	11	12
THU	01	02	03	04	05	06	07	08	09	10	11	12
FRI	01	02	03	04	05	06	07	08	09	10	11	12
SAT	01	02	03	04	05	06	07	08	09	10	11	12
SUN	01	02	03	04	05	06	07	08	09	10	11	12
MON	01	02	03	04	05	06	07	08	09	10	11	12
TUE	01	02	03	04	05	06	07	08	09	10	11	12
WED	01	02	03	04	05	06	07	08	09	10	11	12
THU	01	02	03	04	05	06	07	08	09	10	11	12
FRI	01	02	03	04	05	06	07	08	09	10	11	12
SAT	01	02	03	04	05	06	07	08	09	10	11	12
SUN	01	02	03	04	05	06	07	08	09	10	11	12
MON	01	02	03	04	05	06	07	08	09	10	11	12
TUE	01	02	03	04	05	06	07	08	09	10	11	12
WED	01	02	03	04	05	06	07	08	09	10	11	12
THU	01	02	03	04	05	06	07	08	09	10	11	12
FRI	01	02	03	04	05	06	07	08	09	10	11	12
SAT	01	02	03	04	05	06	07	08	09	10	11	12
SUN	01	02	03	04	05	06	07	08	09	10	11	12

NOTES:

DATE I STARTED TRACKING:

DAILY *Awareness*

MONTH:

M T W T F S S

HOW I'M FEELING TODAY

3 WORDS TO DESCRIBE MY DAY

STRUGGLES

HIGHLIGHT OF MY DAY

DAILY ACCOMPLISHMENTS

POST Therapy Chart

DATE:

SUMMARY/OVERVIEW OF THERAPY SESSION

WHAT WE DISCUSSED

HOW IT MADE ME FEEL

WHAT I LEARNED

WHAT I WANT TO DISCUSS NEXT

Rate your session to keep track of progress.

THOUGHTS *Tracker*

MONITORING YOUR THOUGHTS & FEELINGS

MONDAY'S THOUGHTS

TUESDAY'S THOUGHTS

WEDNESDAY'S THOUGHTS

THURSDAY'S THOUGHTS

FRIDAY'S THOUGHTS

SATURDAY'S THOUGHTS

SUNDAY'S THOUGHTS

WEEKLY Assessment

	SLEEP	MOOD	POSITIVES	NEGATIVES
MONDAY				
TUESDAY				
WEDNESDAY				
THURSDAY				
FRIDAY				
SATURDAY				
SUNDAY				

WEEKLY *Reflections*

Monday

Tuesday

Wednesday

Thursday

Friday

Saturday

Sunday

DAILY *Reflection*

DATE:

HOW I FEEL TODAY

MY GREATEST CHALLENGE

MOOD TRACKER:

MORNING:

EVENING:

I FELT HAPPY WHEN:

I FELT EXCITED WHEN:

I FELT ENERGIZED WHEN:

Today's Highlights

What I'm Grateful For Today

DAILY Awareness

MONTH:

M T W T F S S

HOW I'M FEELING TODAY

3 WORDS TO DESCRIBE MY DAY

STRUGGLES

HIGHLIGHT OF MY DAY

DAILY ACCOMPLISHMENTS

DATE:

DAILY *Reflection*

HOW I FEEL TODAY **MY GREATEST CHALLENGE**

MOOD TRACKER:

MORNING: **EVENING:**

I FELT HAPPY WHEN: **I FELT EXCITED WHEN:** **I FELT ENERGIZED WHEN:**

Today's Highlights

What I'm Grateful For Today

DAILY *Awareness*

MONTH:

M T W T F S S

HOW I'M FEELING TODAY

3 WORDS TO DESCRIBE MY DAY

STRUGGLES

HIGHLIGHT OF MY DAY

DAILY ACCOMPLISHMENTS

DAILY *Reflection*

DATE:

HOW I FEEL TODAY

MY GREATEST CHALLENGE

MOOD TRACKER:

MORNING:

EVENING:

I FELT HAPPY WHEN:

I FELT EXCITED WHEN:

I FELT ENERGIZED WHEN:

Today's Highlights

What I'm Grateful For Today

DAILY *Awareness*

MONTH:

M   T   W   T   F   S   S

HOW I'M FEELING TODAY

3 WORDS TO DESCRIBE MY DAY   **STRUGGLES**

HIGHLIGHT OF MY DAY

DAILY ACCOMPLISHMENTS

DATE:

DAILY *Reflection*

HOW I FEEL TODAY **MY GREATEST CHALLENGE**

MOOD TRACKER:

MORNING: **EVENING:**

I FELT HAPPY WHEN: **I FELT EXCITED WHEN:** **I FELT ENERGIZED WHEN:**

Today's Highlights

What I'm Grateful For Today

DAILY *Awareness*

MONTH:

M T W T F S S

HOW I'M FEELING TODAY

3 WORDS TO DESCRIBE MY DAY   **STRUGGLES**

HIGHLIGHT OF MY DAY

DAILY ACCOMPLISHMENTS

DAILY *Reflection*

DATE:

HOW I FEEL TODAY

MY GREATEST CHALLENGE

MOOD TRACKER:

MORNING:

EVENING:

I FELT HAPPY WHEN:

I FELT EXCITED WHEN:

I FELT ENERGIZED WHEN:

Today's Highlights

What I'm Grateful For Today

DAILY *Awareness*

MONTH:

M T W T F S S

HOW I'M FEELING TODAY

3 WORDS TO DESCRIBE MY DAY

STRUGGLES

HIGHLIGHT OF MY DAY

DAILY ACCOMPLISHMENTS

DAILY *Reflection*

DATE:

HOW I FEEL TODAY

MY GREATEST CHALLENGE

MOOD TRACKER:

MORNING:

EVENING:

I FELT HAPPY WHEN:

I FELT EXCITED WHEN:

I FELT ENERGIZED WHEN:

Today's Highlights

What I'm Grateful For Today

DAILY *Awareness*

MONTH:

M T W T F S S

HOW I'M FEELING TODAY

3 WORDS TO DESCRIBE MY DAY   **STRUGGLES**

HIGHLIGHT OF MY DAY

DAILY ACCOMPLISHMENTS

DAILY *Reflection*

DATE:

HOW I FEEL TODAY

MY GREATEST CHALLENGE

MOOD TRACKER:

MORNING:

EVENING:

I FELT HAPPY WHEN:

I FELT EXCITED WHEN:

I FELT ENERGIZED WHEN:

Today's Highlights

What I'm Grateful For Today

DAILY *Awareness*

MONTH:

M T W T F S S

HOW I'M FEELING TODAY

3 WORDS TO DESCRIBE MY DAY **STRUGGLES**

HIGHLIGHT OF MY DAY

DAILY ACCOMPLISHMENTS

POST Therapy Chart

DATE:

SUMMARY/OVERVIEW OF THERAPY SESSION

WHAT WE DISCUSSED

HOW IT MADE ME FEEL

WHAT I LEARNED

WHAT I WANT TO DISCUSS NEXT

Rate your session to keep track of progress.

THOUGHTS *Tracker*

MONITORING YOUR THOUGHTS & FEELINGS

MONDAY'S THOUGHTS

TUESDAY'S THOUGHTS

WEDNESDAY'S THOUGHTS

THURSDAY'S THOUGHTS

FRIDAY'S THOUGHTS

SATURDAY'S THOUGHTS

SUNDAY'S THOUGHTS

WEEKLY Assessment

	SLEEP	MOOD	POSITIVES	NEGATIVES
MONDAY				
TUESDAY				
WEDNESDAY				
THURSDAY				
FRIDAY				
SATURDAY				
SUNDAY				

WEEKLY *Reflections*

Monday

Tuesday

Wednesday

Thursday

Friday

Saturday

Sunday

DAILY Reflection

DATE:

HOW I FEEL TODAY

MY GREATEST CHALLENGE

MOOD TRACKER:

MORNING:

EVENING:

I FELT HAPPY WHEN:

I FELT EXCITED WHEN:

I FELT ENERGIZED WHEN:

Today's Highlights

What I'm Grateful For Today

DAILY Awareness

MONTH:

M T W T F S S

HOW I'M FEELING TODAY

3 WORDS TO DESCRIBE MY DAY

STRUGGLES

HIGHLIGHT OF MY DAY

DAILY ACCOMPLISHMENTS

DATE:

DAILY Reflection

HOW I FEEL TODAY **MY GREATEST CHALLENGE**

MOOD TRACKER:

MORNING: **EVENING:**

I FELT HAPPY WHEN: **I FELT EXCITED WHEN:** **I FELT ENERGIZED WHEN:**

Today's Highlights

What I'm Grateful For Today

DAILY *Awareness*

MONTH:

M T W T F S S

HOW I'M FEELING TODAY

3 WORDS TO DESCRIBE MY DAY **STRUGGLES**

HIGHLIGHT OF MY DAY

DAILY ACCOMPLISHMENTS

DATE:

DAILY *Reflection*

HOW I FEEL TODAY   **MY GREATEST CHALLENGE**

MOOD TRACKER:

MORNING: **EVENING:**

I FELT HAPPY WHEN: **I FELT EXCITED WHEN:**   **I FELT ENERGIZED WHEN:**

Today's Highlights

What I'm Grateful For Today

DAILY Awareness

MONTH:

M T W T F S S

HOW I'M FEELING TODAY

3 WORDS TO DESCRIBE MY DAY

STRUGGLES

HIGHLIGHT OF MY DAY

DAILY ACCOMPLISHMENTS

DAILY *Reflection*

DATE:

HOW I FEEL TODAY

MY GREATEST CHALLENGE

MOOD TRACKER:

MORNING:

EVENING:

I FELT HAPPY WHEN:

I FELT EXCITED WHEN:

I FELT ENERGIZED WHEN:

Today's Highlights

What I'm Grateful For Today

DAILY *Awareness*

MONTH:

M T W T F S S

HOW I'M FEELING TODAY

3 WORDS TO DESCRIBE MY DAY

STRUGGLES

HIGHLIGHT OF MY DAY

DAILY ACCOMPLISHMENTS

DAILY *Reflection*

DATE:

HOW I FEEL TODAY

MY GREATEST CHALLENGE

MOOD TRACKER:

MORNING:

EVENING:

I FELT HAPPY WHEN:

I FELT EXCITED WHEN:

I FELT ENERGIZED WHEN:

Today's Highlights

What I'm Grateful For Today

DAILY *Awareness*

MONTH:

M T W T F S S

HOW I'M FEELING TODAY

3 WORDS TO DESCRIBE MY DAY

STRUGGLES

HIGHLIGHT OF MY DAY

DAILY ACCOMPLISHMENTS

DAILY *Reflection*

DATE:

HOW I FEEL TODAY

MY GREATEST CHALLENGE

MOOD TRACKER:

MORNING:

EVENING:

I FELT HAPPY WHEN:

I FELT EXCITED WHEN:

I FELT ENERGIZED WHEN:

Today's Highlights

What I'm Grateful For Today

DAILY *Awareness*

MONTH:

M T W T F S S

HOW I'M FEELING TODAY

3 WORDS TO DESCRIBE MY DAY

STRUGGLES

HIGHLIGHT OF MY DAY

DAILY ACCOMPLISHMENTS

DATE:

DAILY *Reflection*

HOW I FEEL TODAY **MY GREATEST CHALLENGE**

MOOD TRACKER:

MORNING: EVENING:

I FELT HAPPY WHEN: **I FELT EXCITED WHEN:** **I FELT ENERGIZED WHEN:**

Today's Highlights

What I'm Grateful For Today

DAILY *Awareness*

MONTH:

M T W T F S S

HOW I'M FEELING TODAY

3 WORDS TO DESCRIBE MY DAY   **STRUGGLES**

HIGHLIGHT OF MY DAY

DAILY ACCOMPLISHMENTS

POST Therapy Chart

DATE:

SUMMARY/OVERVIEW OF THERAPY SESSION

WHAT WE DISCUSSED

HOW IT MADE ME FEEL

WHAT I LEARNED

WHAT I WANT TO DISCUSS NEXT

Rate your session to keep track of progress.

THOUGHTS *Tracker*

MONITORING YOUR THOUGHTS & FEELINGS

MONDAY'S THOUGHTS

TUESDAY'S THOUGHTS

WEDNESDAY'S THOUGHTS

THURSDAY'S THOUGHTS

FRIDAY'S THOUGHTS

SATURDAY'S THOUGHTS

SUNDAY'S THOUGHTS

WEEKLY Assessment

	SLEEP	MOOD	POSITIVES	NEGATIVES
MONDAY				
TUESDAY				
WEDNESDAY				
THURSDAY				
FRIDAY				
SATURDAY				
SUNDAY				

WEEKLY *Reflections*

Monday

Tuesday

Wednesday

Thursday

Friday

Saturday

Sunday

DAILY *Reflection*

DATE:

HOW I FEEL TODAY

MY GREATEST CHALLENGE

MOOD TRACKER:

MORNING:

EVENING:

I FELT HAPPY WHEN:

I FELT EXCITED WHEN:

I FELT ENERGIZED WHEN:

Today's Highlights

What I'm Grateful For Today

DAILY *Awareness*

MONTH:

M T W T F S S

HOW I'M FEELING TODAY

3 WORDS TO DESCRIBE MY DAY

STRUGGLES

HIGHLIGHT OF MY DAY

DAILY ACCOMPLISHMENTS

DATE:

DAILY *Reflection*

HOW I FEEL TODAY **MY GREATEST CHALLENGE**

MOOD TRACKER:

MORNING: **EVENING:**

I FELT HAPPY WHEN: **I FELT EXCITED WHEN:** **I FELT ENERGIZED WHEN:**

Today's Highlights

What I'm Grateful For Today

DAILY Awareness

MONTH:

M T W T F S S

HOW I'M FEELING TODAY

3 WORDS TO DESCRIBE MY DAY

STRUGGLES

HIGHLIGHT OF MY DAY

DAILY ACCOMPLISHMENTS

DATE:

DAILY Reflection

HOW I FEEL TODAY

MY GREATEST CHALLENGE

MOOD TRACKER:

MORNING:

EVENING:

I FELT HAPPY WHEN:

I FELT EXCITED WHEN:

I FELT ENERGIZED WHEN:

Today's Highlights

What I'm Grateful For Today

DAILY *Awareness*

MONTH:

M T W T F S S

HOW I'M FEELING TODAY

3 WORDS TO DESCRIBE MY DAY   **STRUGGLES**

HIGHLIGHT OF MY DAY

DAILY ACCOMPLISHMENTS

DATE:

DAILY Reflection

HOW I FEEL TODAY   **MY GREATEST CHALLENGE**

MOOD TRACKER:

MORNING: EVENING:

I FELT HAPPY WHEN: **I FELT EXCITED WHEN:**   **I FELT ENERGIZED WHEN:**

Today's Highlights

What I'm Grateful For Today

DAILY *Awareness*

MONTH:

M T W T F S S

HOW I'M FEELING TODAY

3 WORDS TO DESCRIBE MY DAY

STRUGGLES

HIGHLIGHT OF MY DAY

DAILY ACCOMPLISHMENTS

DATE:

DAILY *Reflection*

HOW I FEEL TODAY **MY GREATEST CHALLENGE**

MOOD TRACKER:

MORNING: **EVENING:**

I FELT HAPPY WHEN: **I FELT EXCITED WHEN:** **I FELT ENERGIZED WHEN:**

Today's Highlights

What I'm Grateful For Today

DAILY *Awareness*

MONTH:

M T W T F S S

HOW I'M FEELING TODAY

3 WORDS TO DESCRIBE MY DAY

STRUGGLES

HIGHLIGHT OF MY DAY

DAILY ACCOMPLISHMENTS

DATE:

DAILY Reflection

HOW I FEEL TODAY **MY GREATEST CHALLENGE**

MOOD TRACKER:

MORNING: EVENING:

I FELT HAPPY WHEN: I FELT EXCITED WHEN: I FELT ENERGIZED WHEN:

Today's Highlights

What I'm Grateful For Today

DAILY *Awareness*

MONTH:

M T W T F S S

HOW I'M FEELING TODAY

3 WORDS TO DESCRIBE MY DAY **STRUGGLES**

HIGHLIGHT OF MY DAY

DAILY ACCOMPLISHMENTS

DATE:

DAILY Reflection

HOW I FEEL TODAY **MY GREATEST CHALLENGE**

MOOD TRACKER:

MORNING: **EVENING:**

I FELT HAPPY WHEN: **I FELT EXCITED WHEN:** **I FELT ENERGIZED WHEN:**

Today's Highlights

What I'm Grateful For Today

DAILY *Awareness*

MONTH:

M T W T F S S

HOW I'M FEELING TODAY

3 WORDS TO DESCRIBE MY DAY

STRUGGLES

HIGHLIGHT OF MY DAY

DAILY ACCOMPLISHMENTS

POST Therapy Chart

DATE:

SUMMARY/OVERVIEW OF THERAPY SESSION

WHAT WE DISCUSSED

HOW IT MADE ME FEEL

WHAT I LEARNED

WHAT I WANT TO DISCUSS NEXT

Rate your session to keep track of progress.

THOUGHTS *Tracker*

MONITORING YOUR THOUGHTS & FEELINGS

MONDAY'S THOUGHTS

TUESDAY'S THOUGHTS

WEDNESDAY'S THOUGHTS

THURSDAY'S THOUGHTS

FRIDAY'S THOUGHTS

SATURDAY'S THOUGHTS

SUNDAY'S THOUGHTS

WEEKLY *Reflections*

Monday

Tuesday

Wednesday

Thursday

Friday

Saturday

Sunday

DATE:

DAILY *Reflection*

HOW I FEEL TODAY **MY GREATEST CHALLENGE**

MOOD TRACKER:

MORNING: **EVENING:**

I FELT HAPPY WHEN: **I FELT EXCITED WHEN:** **I FELT ENERGIZED WHEN:**

Today's Highlights

What I'm Grateful For Today

DAILY *Awareness*

MONTH:

M T W T F S S

HOW I'M FEELING TODAY

3 WORDS TO DESCRIBE MY DAY

STRUGGLES

HIGHLIGHT OF MY DAY

DAILY ACCOMPLISHMENTS

DAILY *Reflection*

DATE:

HOW I FEEL TODAY

MY GREATEST CHALLENGE

MOOD TRACKER:

MORNING:

EVENING:

I FELT HAPPY WHEN:

I FELT EXCITED WHEN:

I FELT ENERGIZED WHEN:

Today's Highlights

What I'm Grateful For Today

DAILY *Awareness*

MONTH:

M T W T F S S

HOW I'M FEELING TODAY

3 WORDS TO DESCRIBE MY DAY

STRUGGLES

HIGHLIGHT OF MY DAY

DAILY ACCOMPLISHMENTS

DATE:

DAILY Reflection

HOW I FEEL TODAY **MY GREATEST CHALLENGE**

MOOD TRACKER:

MORNING: EVENING:

I FELT HAPPY WHEN: **I FELT EXCITED WHEN:** **I FELT ENERGIZED WHEN:**

Today's Highlights

What I'm Grateful For Today

DAILY *Awareness*

MONTH:

M T W T F S S

HOW I'M FEELING TODAY

3 WORDS TO DESCRIBE MY DAY

STRUGGLES

HIGHLIGHT OF MY DAY

DAILY ACCOMPLISHMENTS

DATE:

DAILY *Reflection*

HOW I FEEL TODAY   **MY GREATEST CHALLENGE**

MOOD TRACKER:

MORNING: **EVENING:**

I FELT HAPPY WHEN: **I FELT EXCITED WHEN:**   **I FELT ENERGIZED WHEN:**

Today's Highlights

What I'm Grateful For Today

DAILY *Awareness*

MONTH:

M T W T F S S

HOW I'M FEELING TODAY

3 WORDS TO DESCRIBE MY DAY

STRUGGLES

HIGHLIGHT OF MY DAY

DAILY ACCOMPLISHMENTS

DATE:

DAILY *Reflection*

HOW I FEEL TODAY MY GREATEST CHALLENGE

MOOD TRACKER:

MORNING: EVENING:

I FELT HAPPY WHEN: I FELT EXCITED WHEN: I FELT ENERGIZED WHEN:

Today's Highlights

What I'm Grateful For Today

DAILY *Awareness*

MONTH:

M T W T F S S

HOW I'M FEELING TODAY

3 WORDS TO DESCRIBE MY DAY

STRUGGLES

HIGHLIGHT OF MY DAY

DAILY ACCOMPLISHMENTS

DATE:

DAILY *Reflection*

HOW I FEEL TODAY MY GREATEST CHALLENGE

MOOD TRACKER:

MORNING: EVENING:

I FELT HAPPY WHEN: I FELT EXCITED WHEN: I FELT ENERGIZED WHEN:

Today's Highlights

What I'm Grateful For Today

DAILY *Awareness*

MONTH:

M T W T F S S

HOW I'M FEELING TODAY

3 WORDS TO DESCRIBE MY DAY

STRUGGLES

HIGHLIGHT OF MY DAY

DAILY ACCOMPLISHMENTS

DATE:

DAILY Reflection

HOW I FEEL TODAY **MY GREATEST CHALLENGE**

MOOD TRACKER:

MORNING: EVENING:

I FELT HAPPY WHEN: I FELT EXCITED WHEN: I FELT ENERGIZED WHEN:

Today's Highlights

What I'm Grateful For Today

DAILY *Awareness*

MONTH:

M T W T F S S

HOW I'M FEELING TODAY

3 WORDS TO DESCRIBE MY DAY

STRUGGLES

HIGHLIGHT OF MY DAY

DAILY ACCOMPLISHMENTS

POST Therapy Chart

DATE:

SUMMARY/OVERVIEW OF THERAPY SESSION

WHAT WE DISCUSSED

HOW IT MADE ME FEEL

WHAT I LEARNED

WHAT I WANT TO DISCUSS NEXT

Rate your session to keep track of progress.

THOUGHTS *Tracker*

MONITORING YOUR THOUGHTS & FEELINGS

MONDAY'S THOUGHTS

TUESDAY'S THOUGHTS

WEDNESDAY'S THOUGHTS

THURSDAY'S THOUGHTS

FRIDAY'S THOUGHTS

SATURDAY'S THOUGHTS

SUNDAY'S THOUGHTS

WEEKLY *Reflections*

Monday

Tuesday

Wednesday

Thursday

Friday

Saturday

Sunday

DATE:

DAILY Reflection

HOW I FEEL TODAY **MY GREATEST CHALLENGE**

MOOD TRACKER:

MORNING: EVENING:

I FELT HAPPY WHEN: I FELT EXCITED WHEN: I FELT ENERGIZED WHEN:

Today's Highlights

What I'm Grateful For Today

DAILY *Awareness*

MONTH:

M T W T F S S

HOW I'M FEELING TODAY

3 WORDS TO DESCRIBE MY DAY   **STRUGGLES**

HIGHLIGHT OF MY DAY

DAILY ACCOMPLISHMENTS

DATE:

DAILY Reflection

HOW I FEEL TODAY   **MY GREATEST CHALLENGE**

MOOD TRACKER:

MORNING: **EVENING:**

I FELT HAPPY WHEN: **I FELT EXCITED WHEN:**   **I FELT ENERGIZED WHEN:**

Today's Highlights

What I'm Grateful For Today

DAILY *Awareness*

MONTH:

M T W T F S S

HOW I'M FEELING TODAY

3 WORDS TO DESCRIBE MY DAY

STRUGGLES

HIGHLIGHT OF MY DAY

DAILY ACCOMPLISHMENTS

DAILY *Reflection*

DATE:

HOW I FEEL TODAY

MY GREATEST CHALLENGE

MOOD TRACKER:

MORNING:

EVENING:

I FELT HAPPY WHEN:

I FELT EXCITED WHEN:

I FELT ENERGIZED WHEN:

Today's Highlights

What I'm Grateful For Today

DAILY Awareness

MONTH:

M T W T F S S

HOW I'M FEELING TODAY

3 WORDS TO DESCRIBE MY DAY

STRUGGLES

HIGHLIGHT OF MY DAY

DAILY ACCOMPLISHMENTS

DATE:

DAILY Reflection

HOW I FEEL TODAY **MY GREATEST CHALLENGE**

MOOD TRACKER:

MORNING: **EVENING:**

I FELT HAPPY WHEN: **I FELT EXCITED WHEN:** **I FELT ENERGIZED WHEN:**

Today's Highlights

What I'm Grateful For Today

DAILY *Awareness*

MONTH:

M T W T F S S

HOW I'M FEELING TODAY

3 WORDS TO DESCRIBE MY DAY　　　　　　　　**STRUGGLES**

HIGHLIGHT OF MY DAY

DAILY ACCOMPLISHMENTS

DATE:

DAILY *Reflection*

HOW I FEEL TODAY

MY GREATEST CHALLENGE

MOOD TRACKER:

MORNING: EVENING:

I FELT HAPPY WHEN: **I FELT EXCITED WHEN:** **I FELT ENERGIZED WHEN:**

Today's Highlights

What I'm Grateful For Today

DAILY *Awareness*

MONTH:

M T W T F S S

HOW I'M FEELING TODAY

3 WORDS TO DESCRIBE MY DAY

STRUGGLES

HIGHLIGHT OF MY DAY

DAILY ACCOMPLISHMENTS

DATE:

DAILY *Reflection*

HOW I FEEL TODAY **MY GREATEST CHALLENGE**

MOOD TRACKER:

MORNING: **EVENING:**

I FELT HAPPY WHEN: **I FELT EXCITED WHEN:** **I FELT ENERGIZED WHEN:**

Today's Highlights

What I'm Grateful For Today

DAILY *Awareness*

MONTH:

M T W T F S S

HOW I'M FEELING TODAY

3 WORDS TO DESCRIBE MY DAY

STRUGGLES

HIGHLIGHT OF MY DAY

DAILY ACCOMPLISHMENTS

DATE:

DAILY Reflection

HOW I FEEL TODAY　　　　　　　　　　　**MY GREATEST CHALLENGE**

MOOD TRACKER:

MORNING:　　　　　　　　　　EVENING:

I FELT HAPPY WHEN:　　　　I FELT EXCITED WHEN:　　　　I FELT ENERGIZED WHEN:

Today's Highlights

What I'm Grateful For Today

DAILY *Awareness*

MONTH:

M T W T F S S

HOW I'M FEELING TODAY

3 WORDS TO DESCRIBE MY DAY   **STRUGGLES**

HIGHLIGHT OF MY DAY

DAILY ACCOMPLISHMENTS

POST Therapy Chart

DATE:

SUMMARY/OVERVIEW OF THERAPY SESSION

WHAT WE DISCUSSED

HOW IT MADE ME FEEL

WHAT I LEARNED

WHAT I WANT TO DISCUSS NEXT

Rate your session to keep track of progress.

THOUGHTS Tracker

MONITORING YOUR THOUGHTS & FEELINGS

MONDAY'S THOUGHTS

TUESDAY'S THOUGHTS

WEDNESDAY'S THOUGHTS

THURSDAY'S THOUGHTS

FRIDAY'S THOUGHTS

SATURDAY'S THOUGHTS

SUNDAY'S THOUGHTS

WEEKLY *Reflections*

Monday

Tuesday

Wednesday

Thursday

Friday

Saturday

Sunday

Made in the USA
Las Vegas, NV
02 August 2022